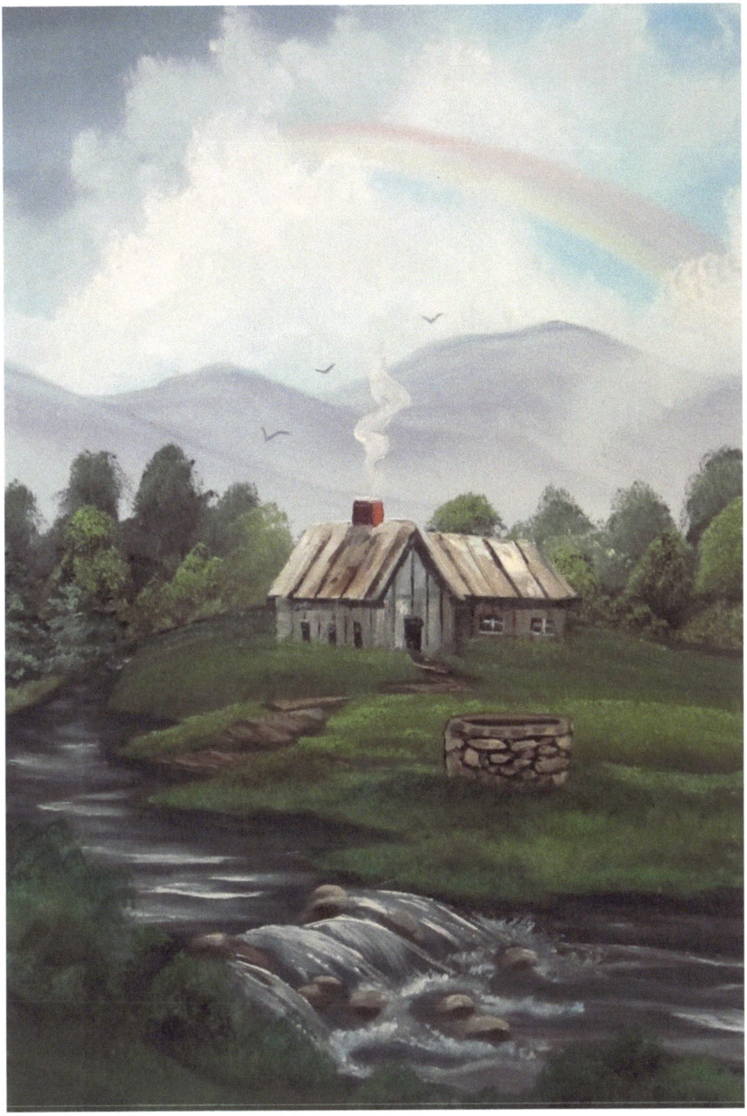

The Art of Hope

The Art of Judith Webb

Other Books by Dirk Webb and Friends Publishing

A Warm Summer's Day

The Next Summer's Day

The Adventures of Mousey Carter McCloud

The Amazing City of Arbella Lamore

Mousey Carter McCloud, Private Eye

Hearing Eyes, Talking Hands: A Child's Questions About Deafness

What Color am I Today?

The Prettiest Psalm: The Art of Judith Webb

Www.dirkwebbandfriends.com

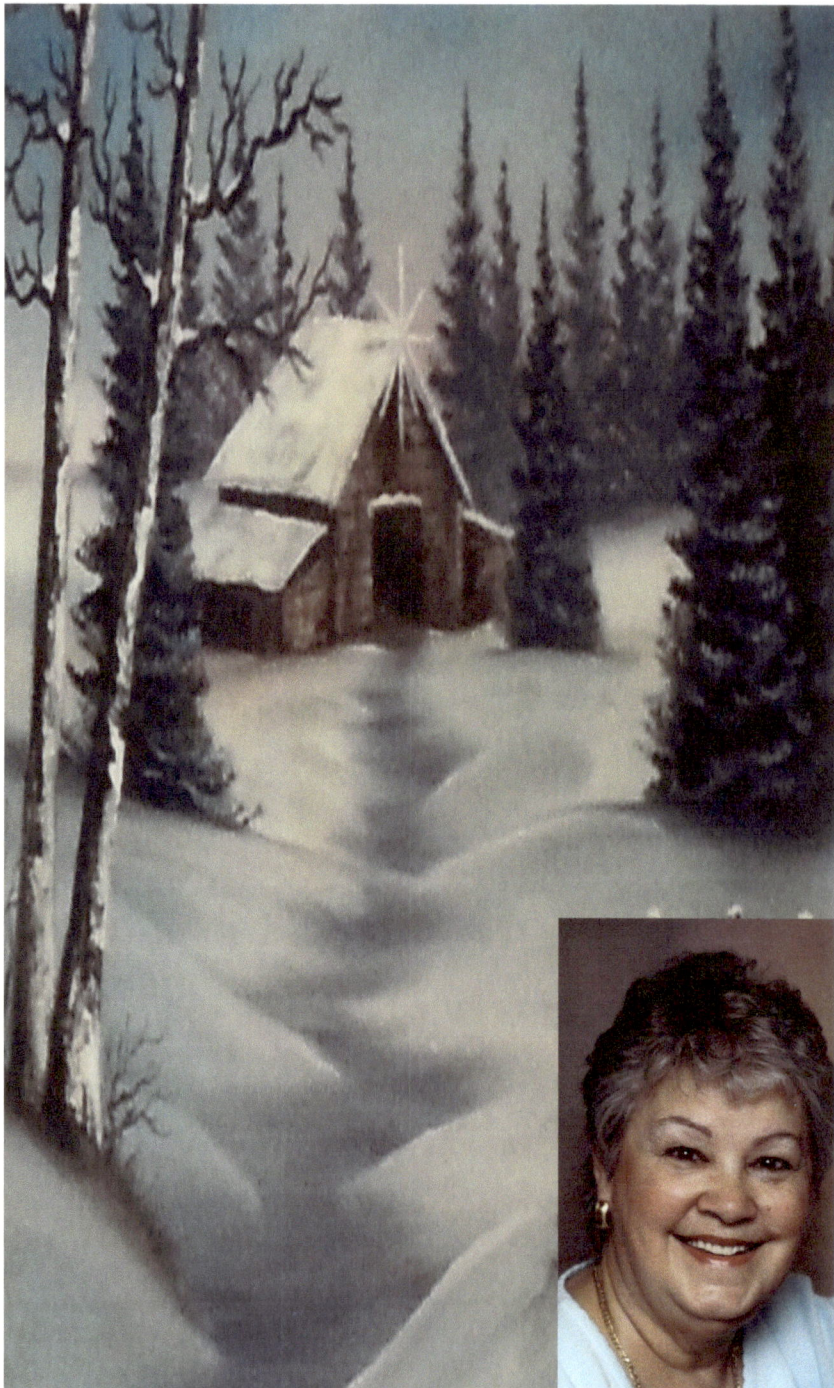

The Art of Hope

This book is lovingly devoted to the memory and art of Judith Webb. Some of us are born to sell, born to build or born to speak. She was a born artist.

From the moment she could hold a pen until the moment she traded her earthly brushes for those eternal, she painted snowy winters, drew summer sunsets and sketched golden autumn.

Most of all, Judith Webb painted hope. Consistent in these pages of her art is a constant theme of abiding confidence in the Creator of Heaven and Earth. She depicted that hope as faithfully as she possibly could and we pray that you will see that expectation rising from each passage and every painting.

We miss her, cherish her memory and

We are ever mindful of hope,

Loyce, Darla and Dirk

2014

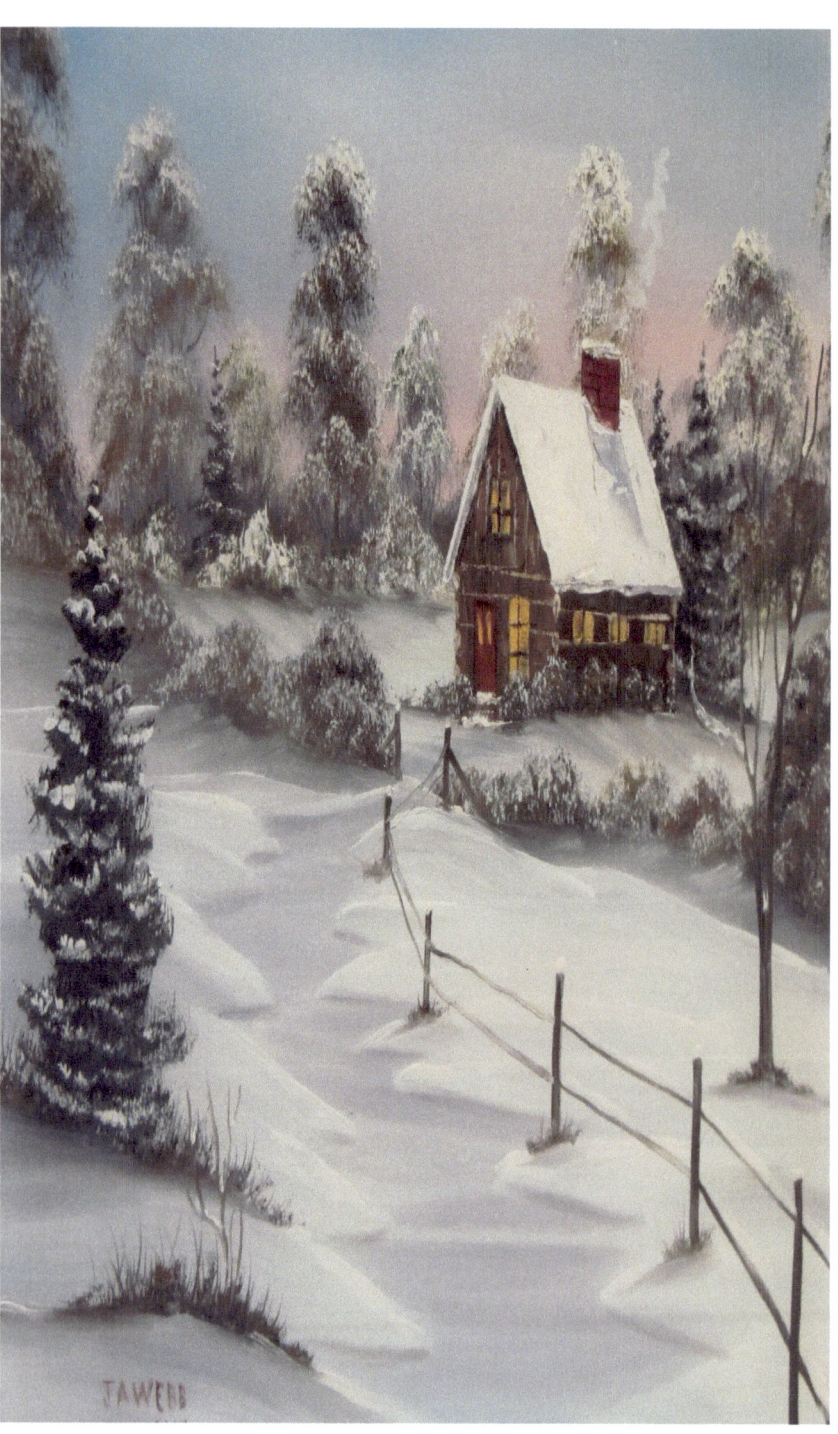

Hope

We are ever mindful of hope.

Without it, we are lost; paralyzed against the vast waves of disappointment, confusion and despair that threaten to overwhelm us every moment of our lives.

With hope, we are immortal; we can conquer any foe, rise to any height and hurdle any obstacle placed before us. Nothing is impossible for us and the world has never been brighter in its long history.

A cherished Bible passage reminds us that "… faith is the substance of things hoped for, the evidence of things not seen." In other words, Hope is that unwavering assurance deep inside us that though all proof points to the contrary, God would never bring us this far to desert us and the answer is just ahead.

We are ever mindful of hope.

When hope fails, we are lost. With hope, we can move the very earth itself.

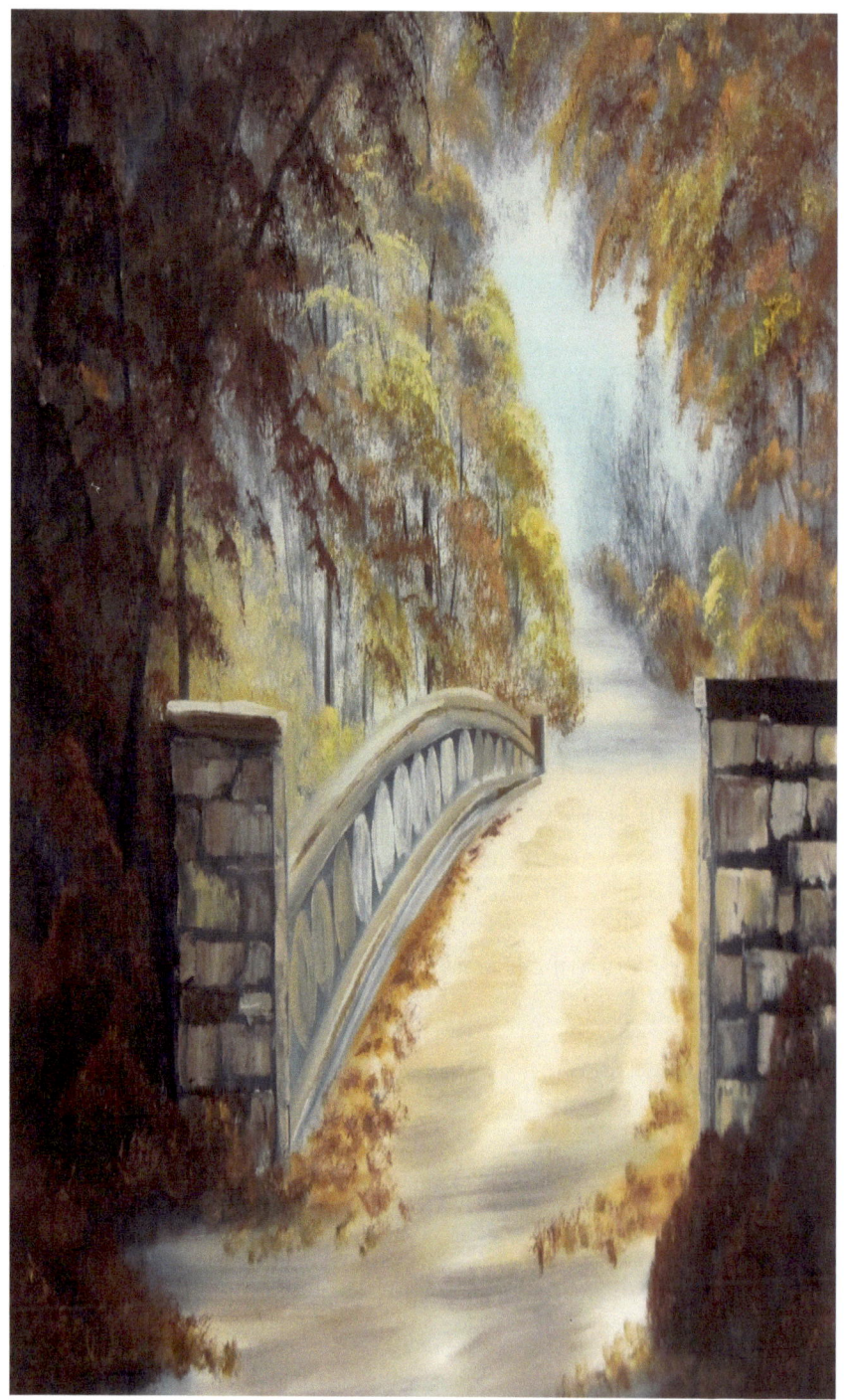

Hebrews 11
New International Version (NIV)

11 Now faith is confidence in what we hope for and assurance about what we do not see. 2 This is what the ancients were commended for. 3 By faith we understand that the universe was formed at God's command, so that what is seen was not made out of what was visible.

Jeremiah 29:11
King James Version (KJV)

11 For I know the thoughts that I think toward you, saith the LORD, thoughts of peace, and not of evil, to give you an expected end.

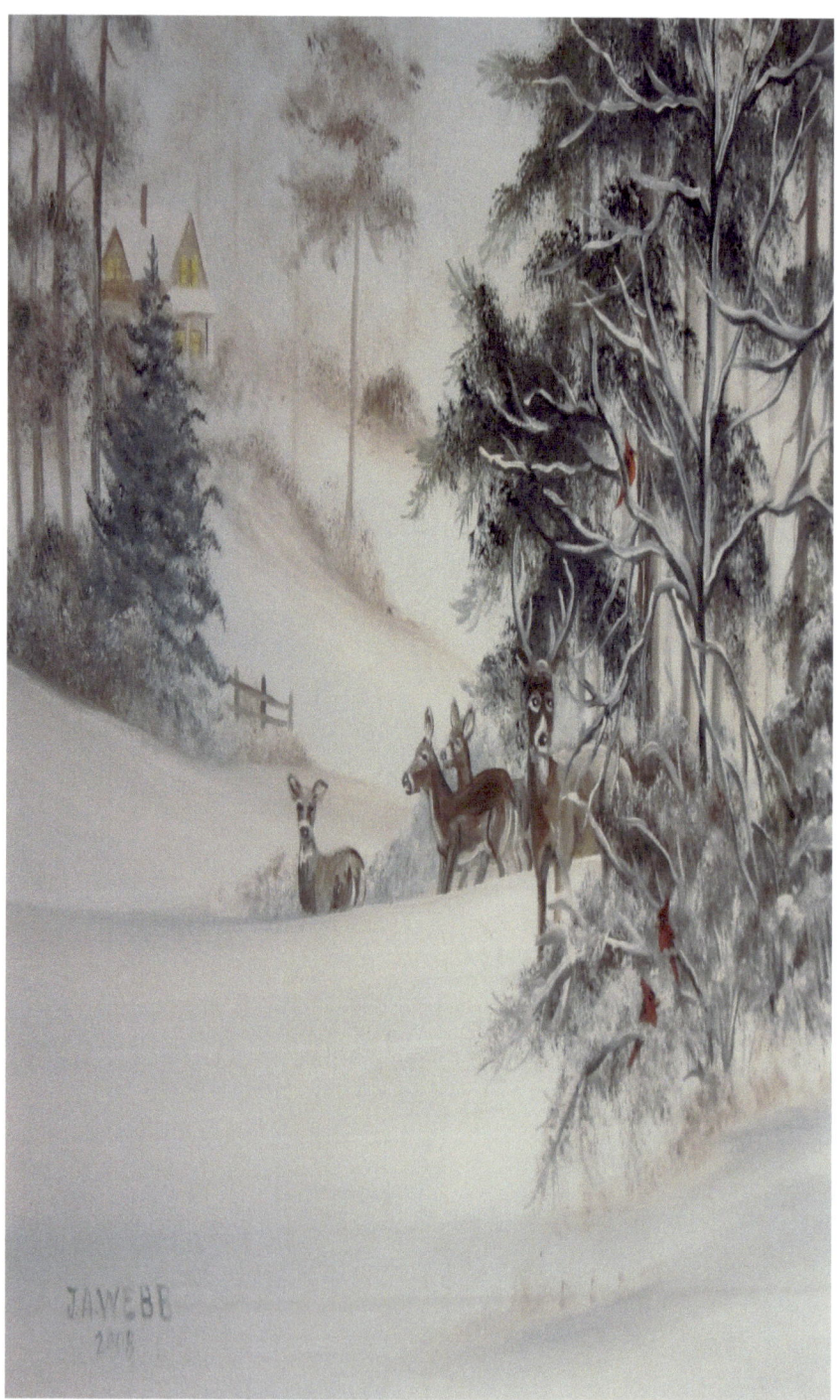

Isaiah 55: 8-9
New International Version (NIV)

[8]"For my thoughts are not your thoughts,
    neither are your ways my ways,"
declares the LORD.
[9] "As the heavens are higher than the earth,
    so are my ways higher than your ways
    and my thoughts than your thoughts.

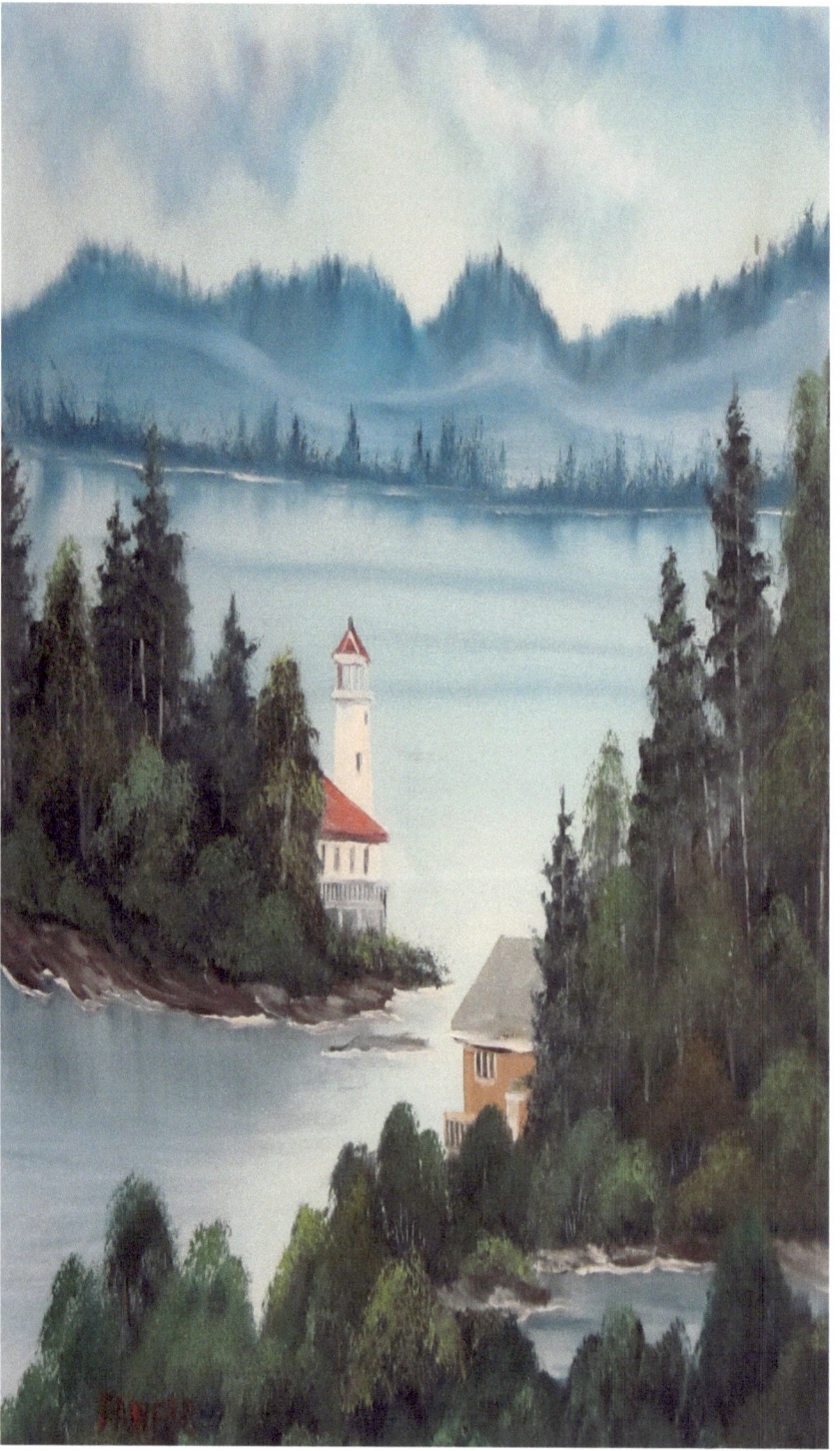

1 Corinthians 2:9
New International Version (NIV)

⁹ However, as it is written:
"What no eye has seen,
　what no ear has heard,
and what no human mind has conceived
　the things God has prepared for those who love
him—

2 Corinthians 4:17-18
New International Version (NIV)

¹⁷ For our light and momentary troubles are achieving for us an eternal glory that far outweighs them all. ¹⁸ So we fix our eyes not on what is seen, but on what is unseen, since what is seen is temporary, but what is unseen is eternal.

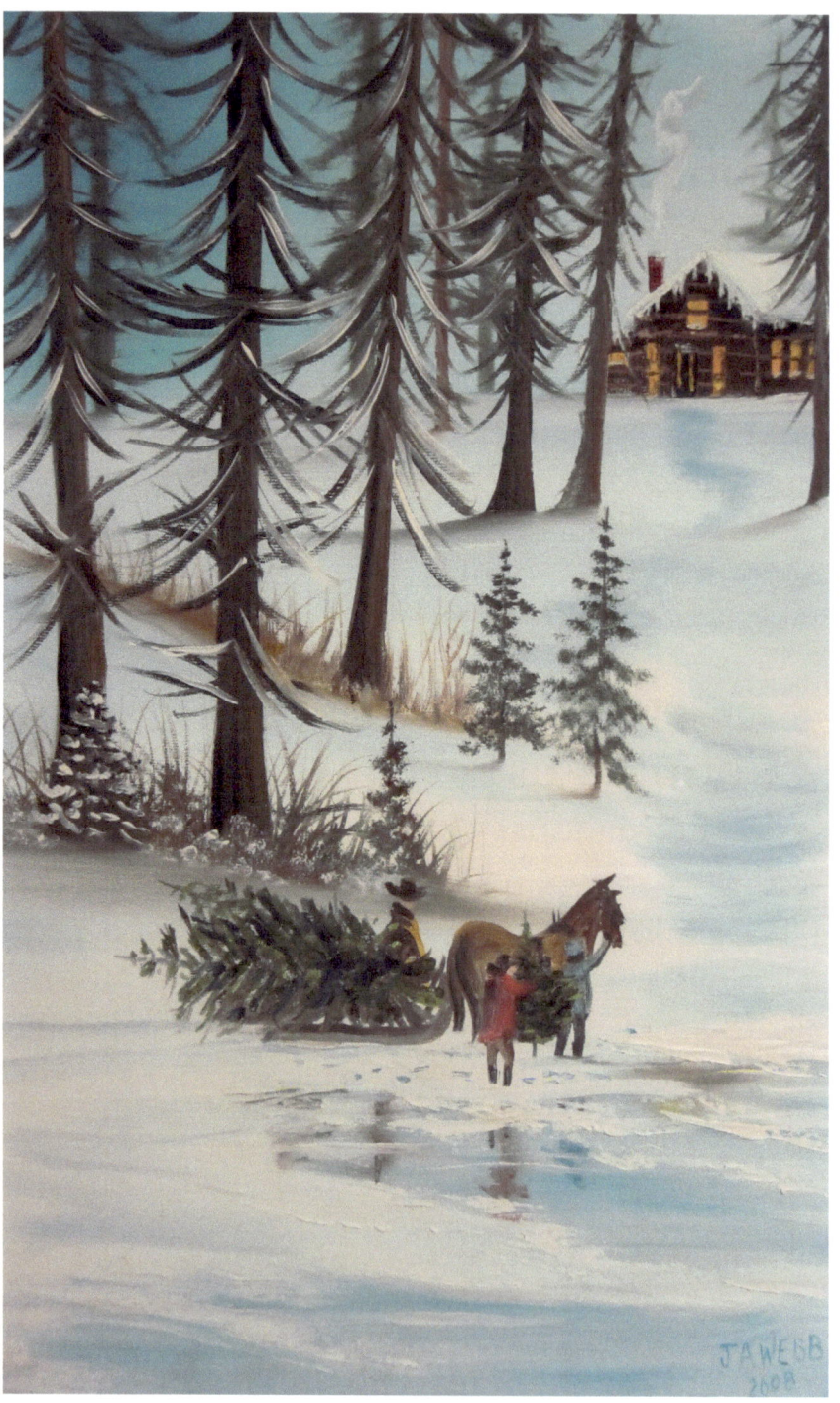

Psalm 149:1-8
New International Version (NIV)

28 "Come to me, all you who are weary and burdened, and I will give you rest.
29 Take my yoke upon you and learn from me, for I am gentle and humble in heart, and you will find rest for your souls.
30 For my yoke is easy and my burden is light."

Proverbs 3:5-6
New International Version (NIV)

5 Trust in the LORD with all your heart
    and lean not on your own understanding;
6 in all your ways submit to him,
    and he will make your paths straight.

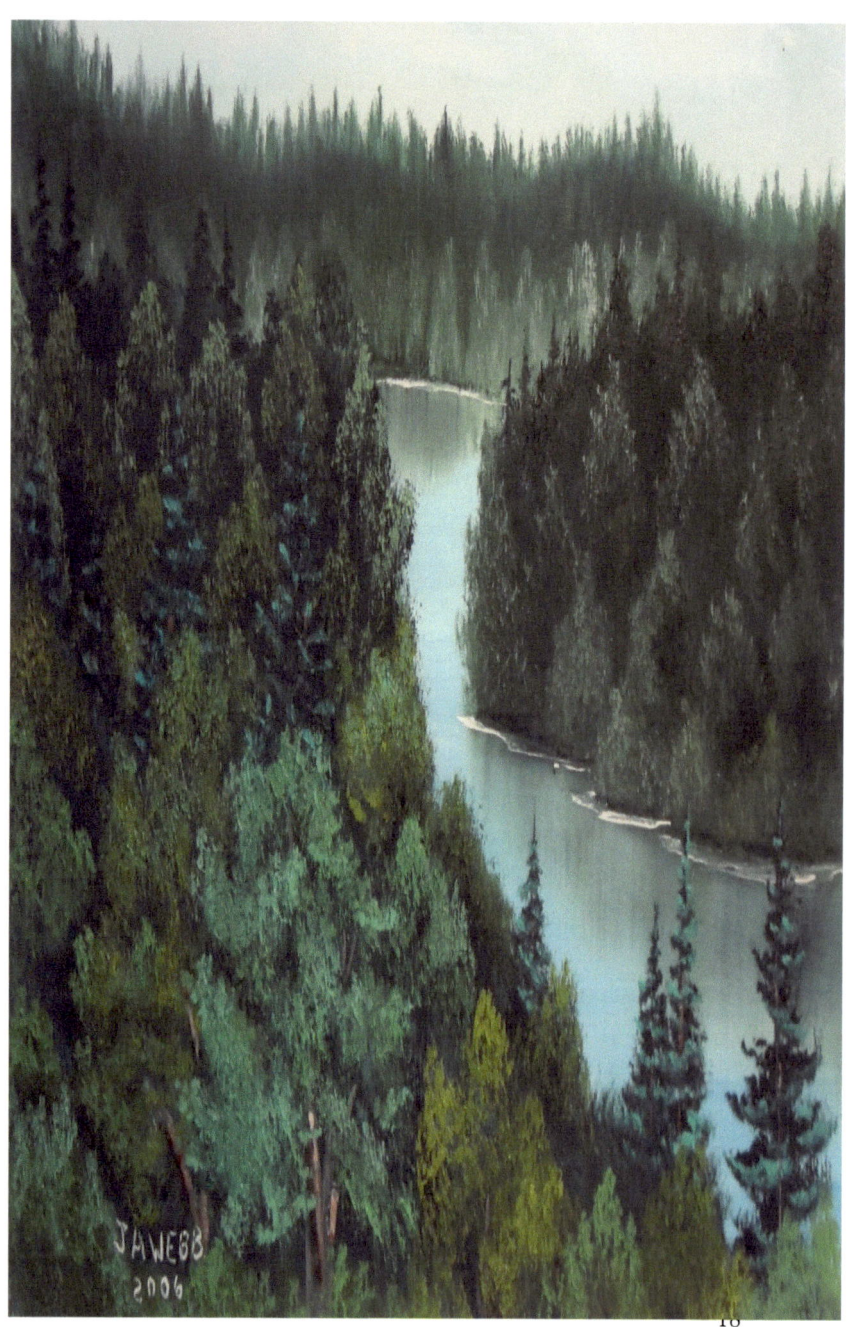

Isaiah 64:4
New International Version (NIV)

4 Since ancient times no one has heard,
    no ear has perceived,
no eye has seen any God besides you,
    who acts on behalf of those who wait for him.

Isaiah 40:31 -

But they that wait upon the LORD shall renew
[their] strength; they shall mount up with wings as
eagles; they shall run, and not be weary; [and] they
shall walk, and not faint.

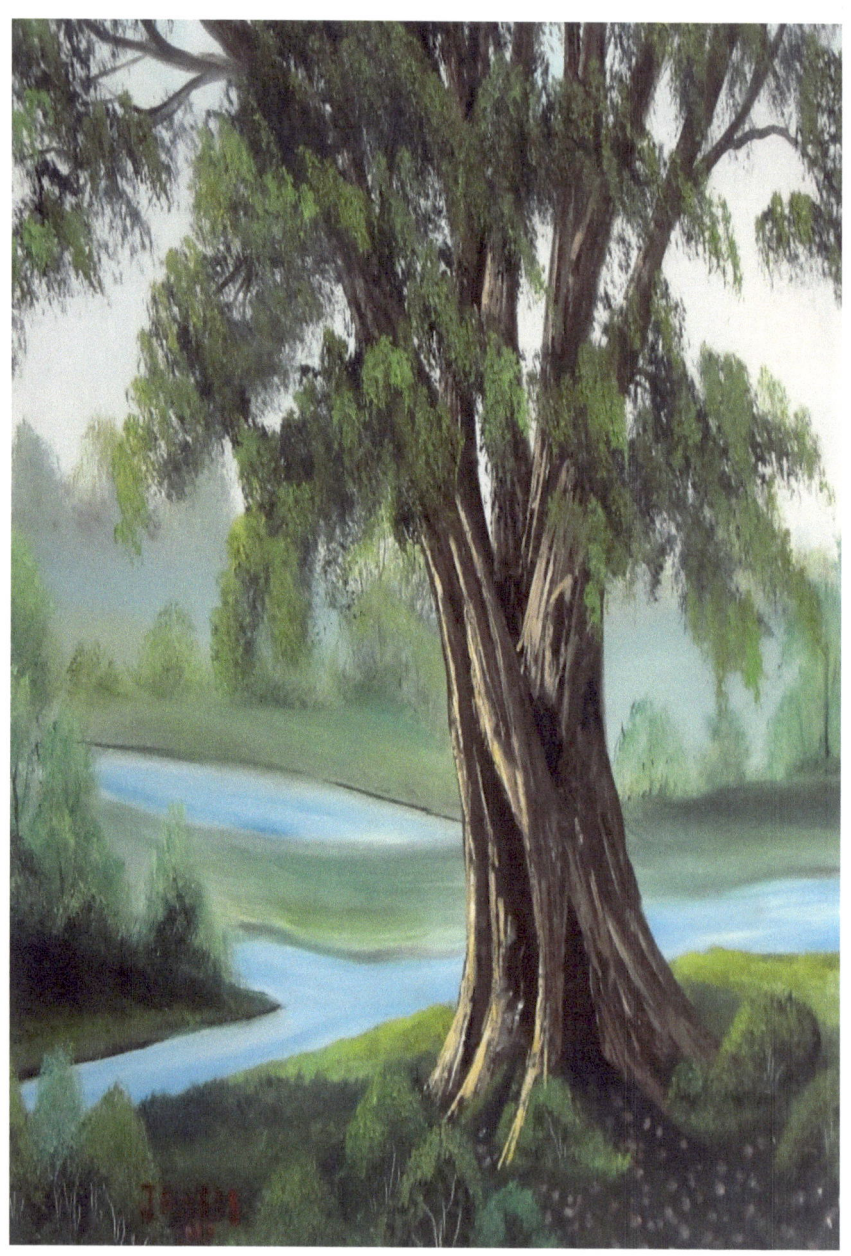

Matthew 5
New International Version (NIV)

Introduction to the Sermon on the Mount

5 Now when Jesus saw the crowds, he went up on a mountainside and sat down. His disciples came to him, **2** and he began to teach them.

The Beatitudes

He said:

3 "Blessed are the poor in spirit,
　for theirs is the kingdom of heaven.
4 Blessed are those who mourn,
　for they will be comforted.
5 Blessed are the meek,
　for they will inherit the earth.
6 Blessed are those who hunger and thirst for righteousness,
　for they will be filled.
7 Blessed are the merciful,
　for they will be shown mercy.
8 Blessed are the pure in heart,
　for they will see God.
9 Blessed are the peacemakers,
　for they will be called children of God.
10 Blessed are those who are persecuted because of righteousness,
　for theirs is the kingdom of heaven.
11 "Blessed are you when people insult you, persecute you and falsely say all kinds of evil against you because of me.
12 Rejoice and be glad, because great is your reward in heaven, for in the same way they persecuted the prophets who were before you.

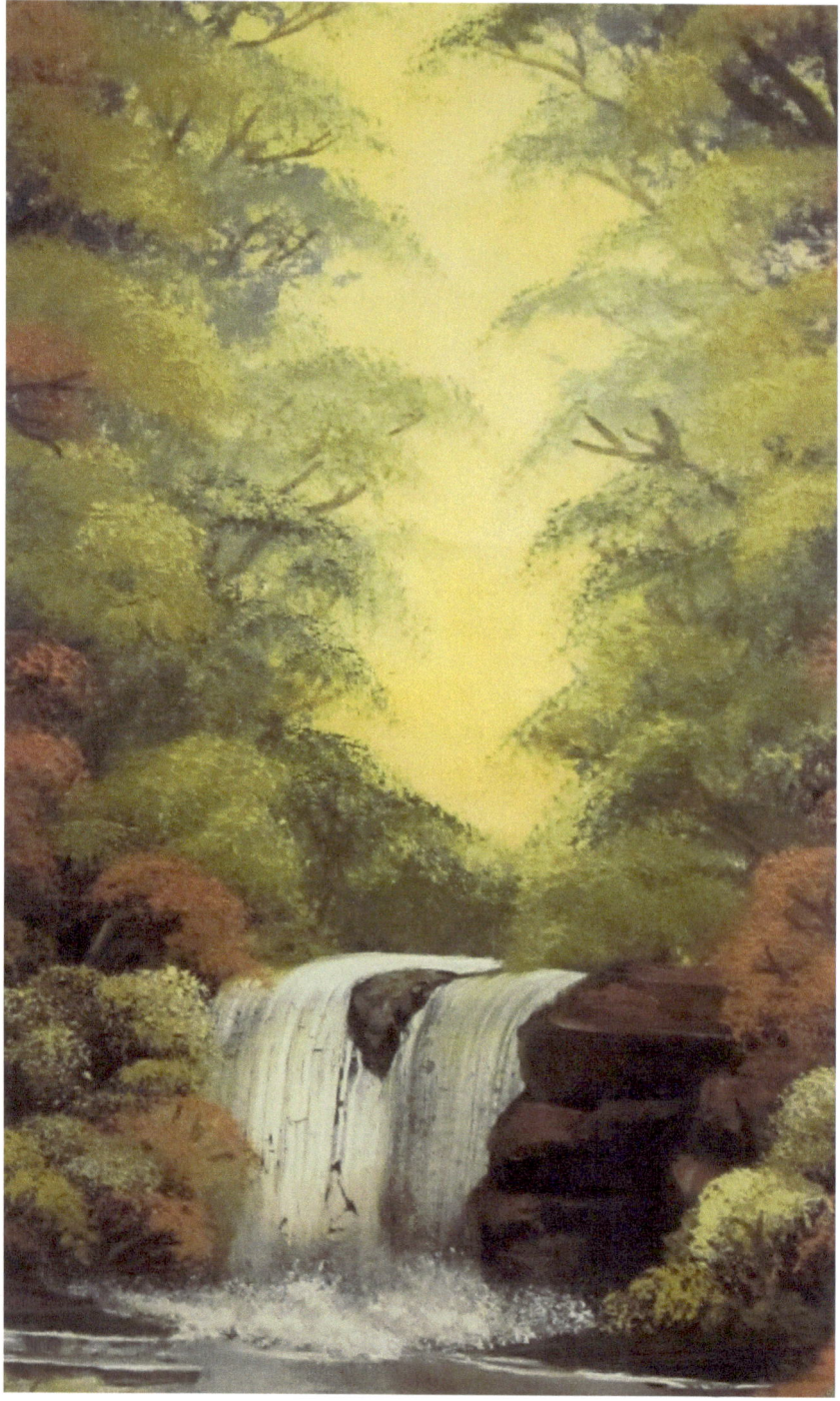

Isaiah 41:10
New International Version (NIV)

[10] So do not fear, for I am with you;
   do not be dismayed, for I am your God.
I will strengthen you and help you;
   I will uphold you with my righteous right hand.

Romans 8:38-39
New International Version (NIV)

[38] For I am convinced that neither death nor life, neither angels nor demons neither the present nor the future, nor any powers,
[39] neither height nor depth, nor anything else in all creation, will be able to separate us from the love of God that is in Christ Jesus our Lord.

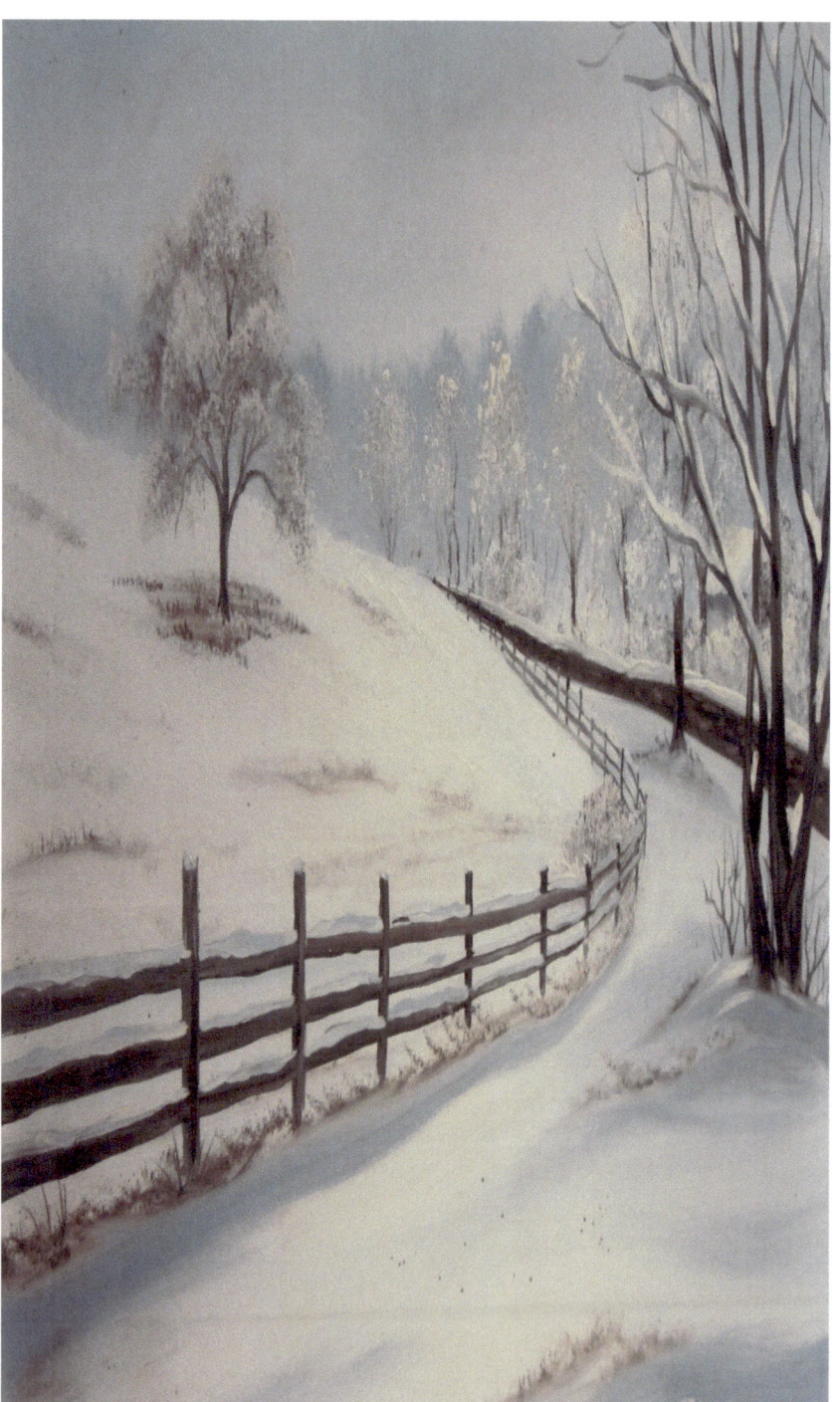

Psalm 42:5

Why are you cast down, O my soul,
    and why are you disquieted within me?
Hope in God; for I shall again praise him,
my help and my God.

Romans 15:13

May the God of hope fill you with all joy and
peace in believing, so that by the power of the
Holy Spirit you may abound in hope.

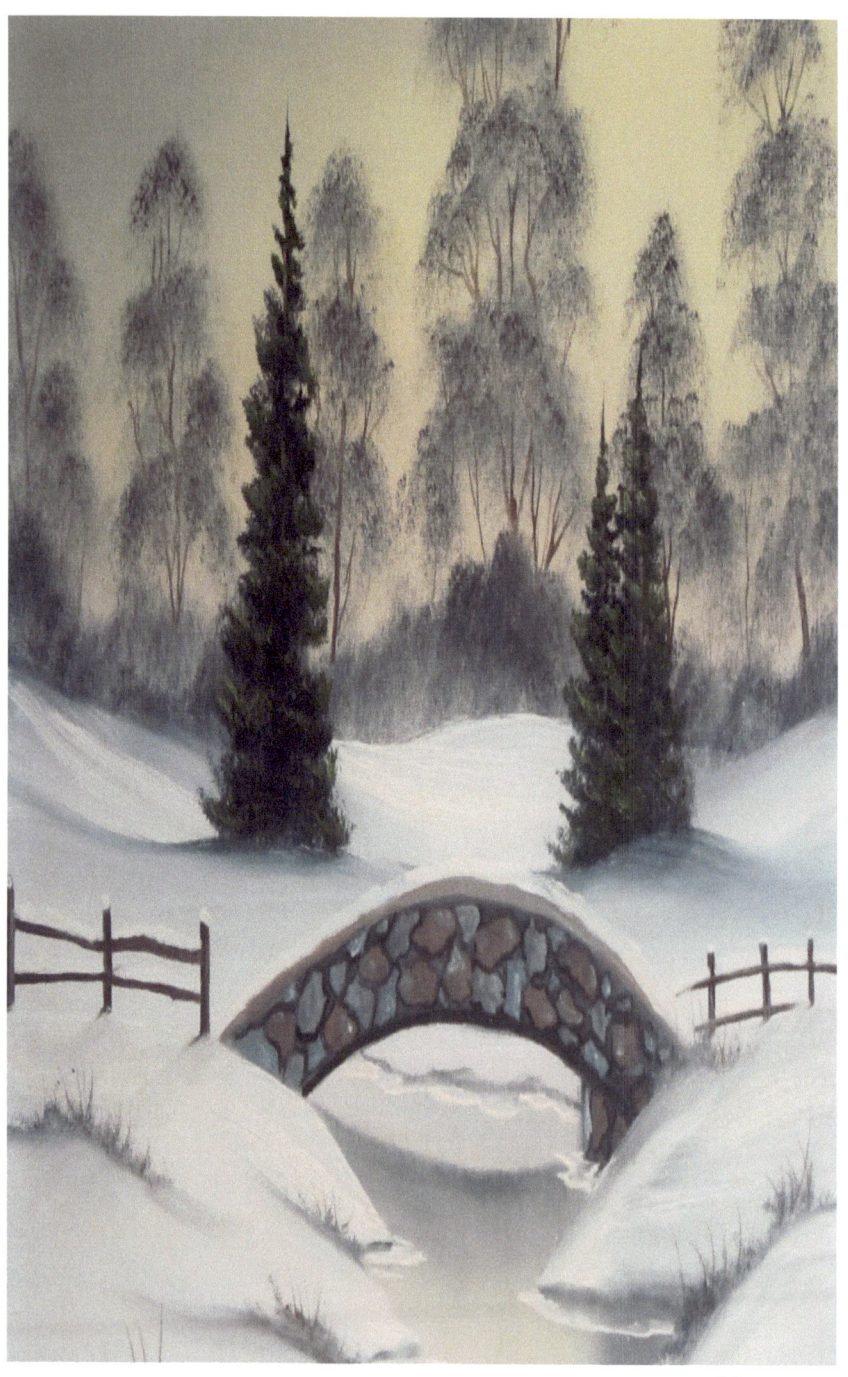

Psalm 118:14-16
New International Version (NIV)

14 The LORD is my strength and my defense;
   he has become my salvation.
15 Shouts of joy and victory
   resound in the tents of the righteous:
"The LORD's right hand has done mighty things!
16   The LORD's right hand is lifted high;
   the LORD's right hand has done mighty things!"

Psalm 27:4
New International Version (NIV)

4 One thing I ask from the LORD,
   this only do I seek:
that I may dwell in the house of the LORD
7   all the days of my life,
to gaze on the beauty of the LORD
   and to seek him in his temple.

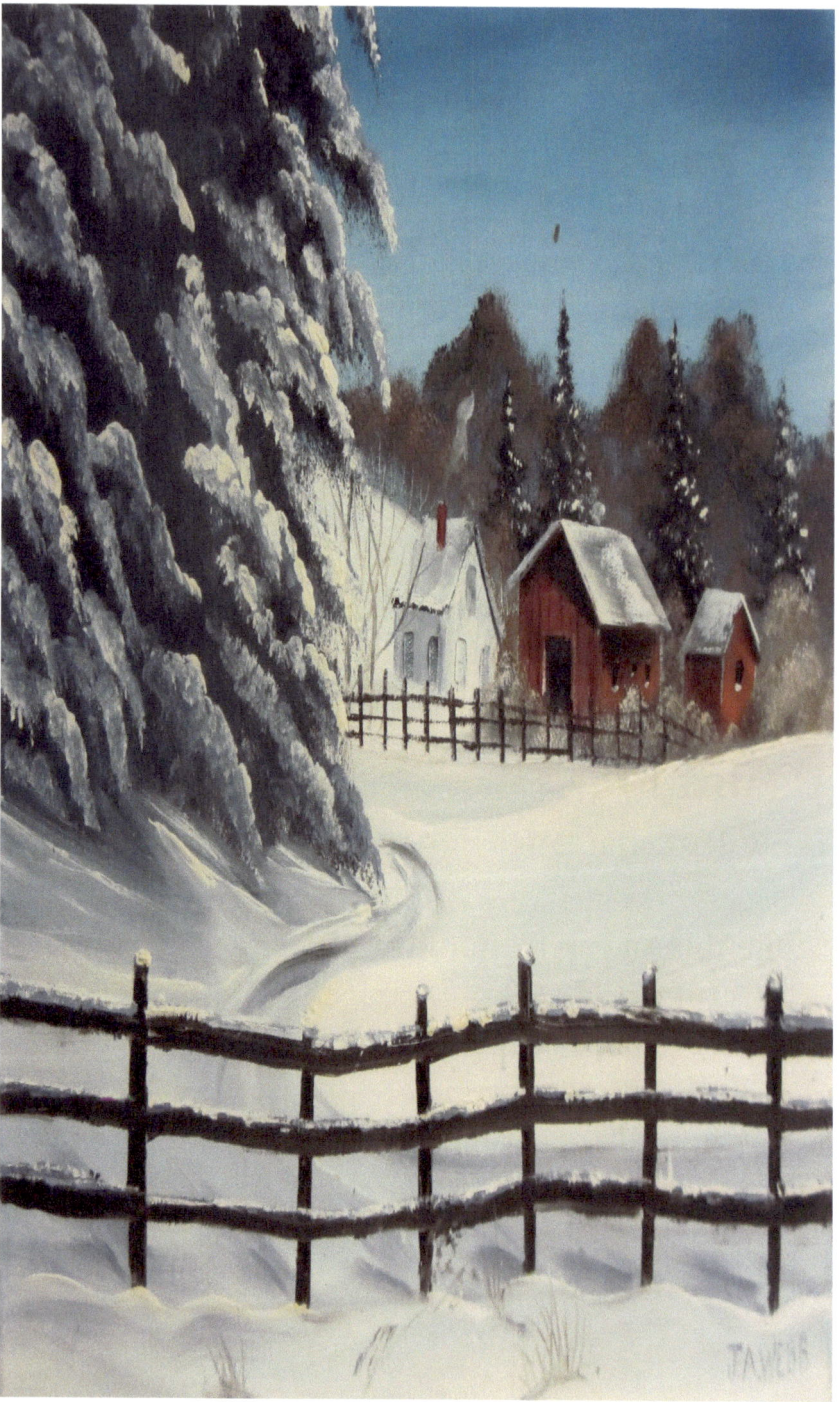

1 Peter 1:3
New International Version (NIV)

3 Praise be to the God and Father of our Lord Jesus Christ! In his great mercy he has given us new birth into a living hope through the resurrection of Jesus Christ from the dead,

Romans 5:2-5
New International Version (NIV)

2 through whom we have gained access by faith into this grace in which we now stand. And we[a] boast in the hope of the glory of God. 3 Not only so, but we also glory in our sufferings, because we know that suffering produces perseverance; 4 perseverance, character; and character, hope. 5 And hope does not put us to shame, because God's love has been poured out into our hearts through the Holy Spirit, who has been given to us.

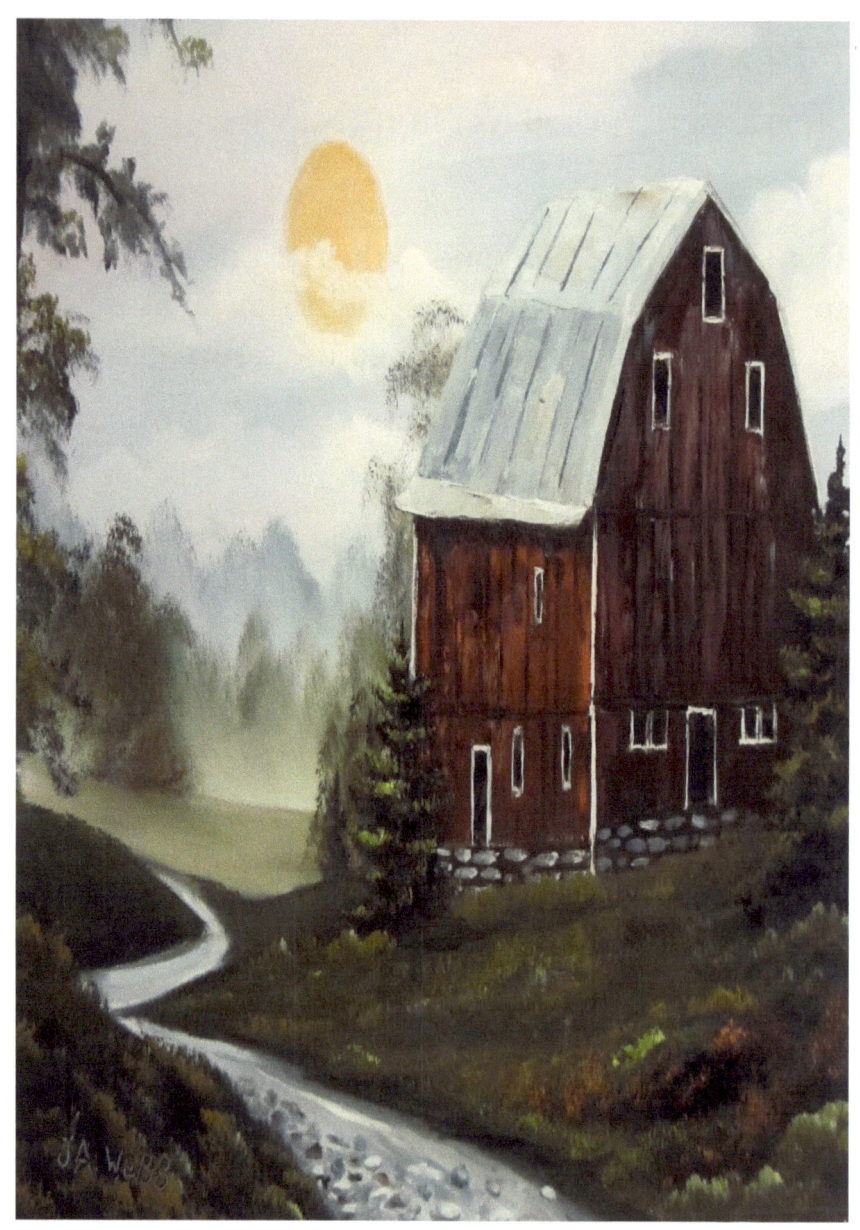

Revelation 21: 1-7
King James Version (KJV)

21 And I saw a new heaven and a new earth: for the first heaven and the first earth were passed away; and there was no more sea.

2 And I John saw the holy city, new Jerusalem, coming down from God out of heaven, prepared as a bride adorned for her husband.

3 And I heard a great voice out of heaven saying, Behold, the tabernacle of God is with men, and he will dwell with them, and they shall be his people, and God himself shall be with them, and be their God.

4 And God shall wipe away all tears from their eyes; and there shall be no more death, neither sorrow, nor crying, neither shall there be any more pain: for the former things are passed away.

5 And he that sat upon the throne said, Behold, I make all things new. And he said unto me, Write: for these words are true and faithful.

6 And he said unto me, It is done. I am Alpha and Omega, the beginning and the end. I will give unto him that is athirst of the fountain of the water of life freely.

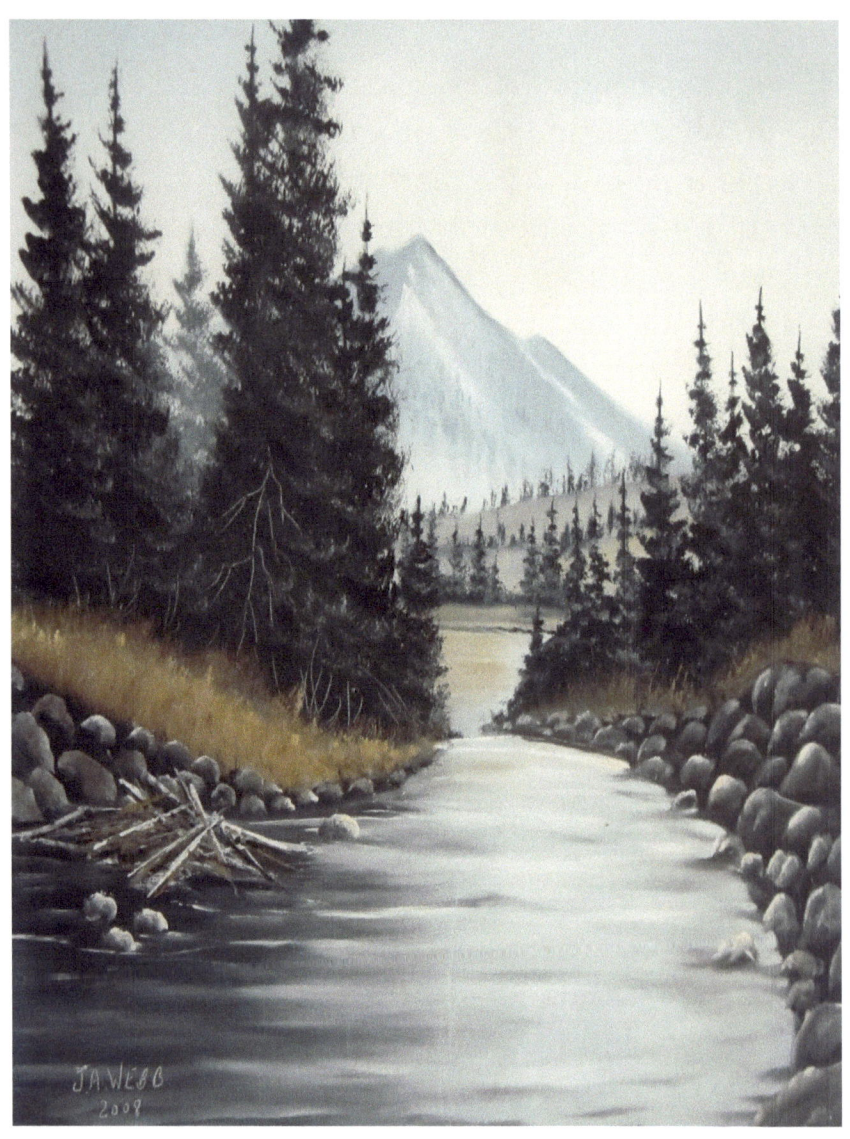

Revelation 22
King James Version (KJV)

22 And he shewed me a pure river of water of life, clear as crystal, proceeding out of the throne of God and of the Lamb.

² In the midst of the street of it, and on either side of the river, was there the tree of life, which bare twelve manner of fruits, and yielded her fruit every month: and the leaves of the tree were for the healing of the nations.

³ And there shall be no more curse: but the throne of God and of the Lamb shall be in it; and his servants shall serve him:

⁴ And they shall see his face; and his name shall be in their foreheads.

⁵ And there shall be no night there; and they need no candle, neither light of the sun; for the Lord God giveth them light: and they shall reign for ever and ever.

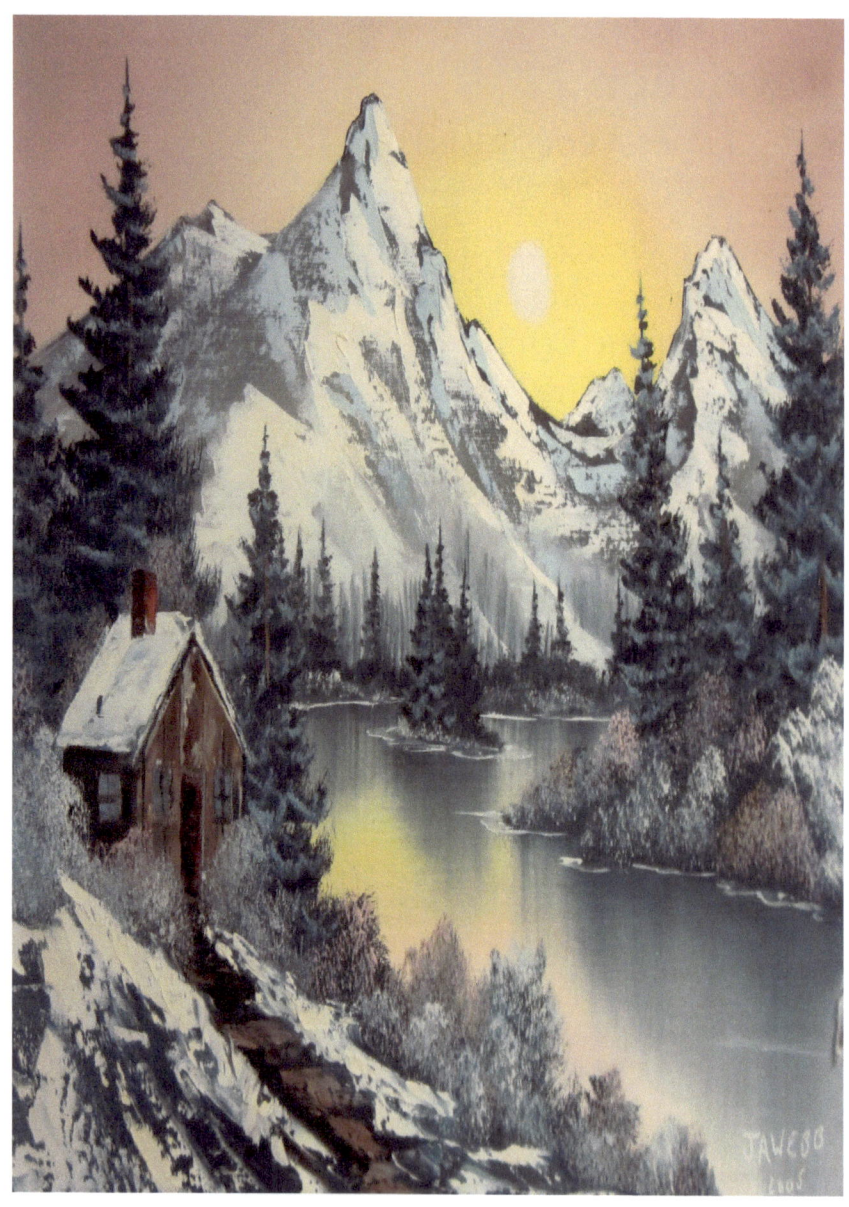

34

The Art of Hope

In the previous scripture, Revelation 22:5, the beloved disciple John wrote, "...And there shall be no night there; and they need no candle, neither light of the sun; for the Lord God giveth them light: and they shall reign forever and ever."

Throughout this book scriptures have described the vast contrast between hope and being without it. When we are without hope, night seems eternal. When we are without hope, we seem to search continually for a light to help us out of that darkness.

John writes that one of the promises of God for our future is there will be no night for God himself is light. If we also know that in God there is no time, shouldn't that promise for light be now as well as in the future?

If you are struggling today without hope, don't give up. While it doesn't seem to be fashionable in our world to do so, maybe it is time to call upon the creator of light.

2 Timothy 1:7
King James Version (KJV)

[7] For God hath not given us the spirit of fear; but of power, and of love, and of a sound mind.

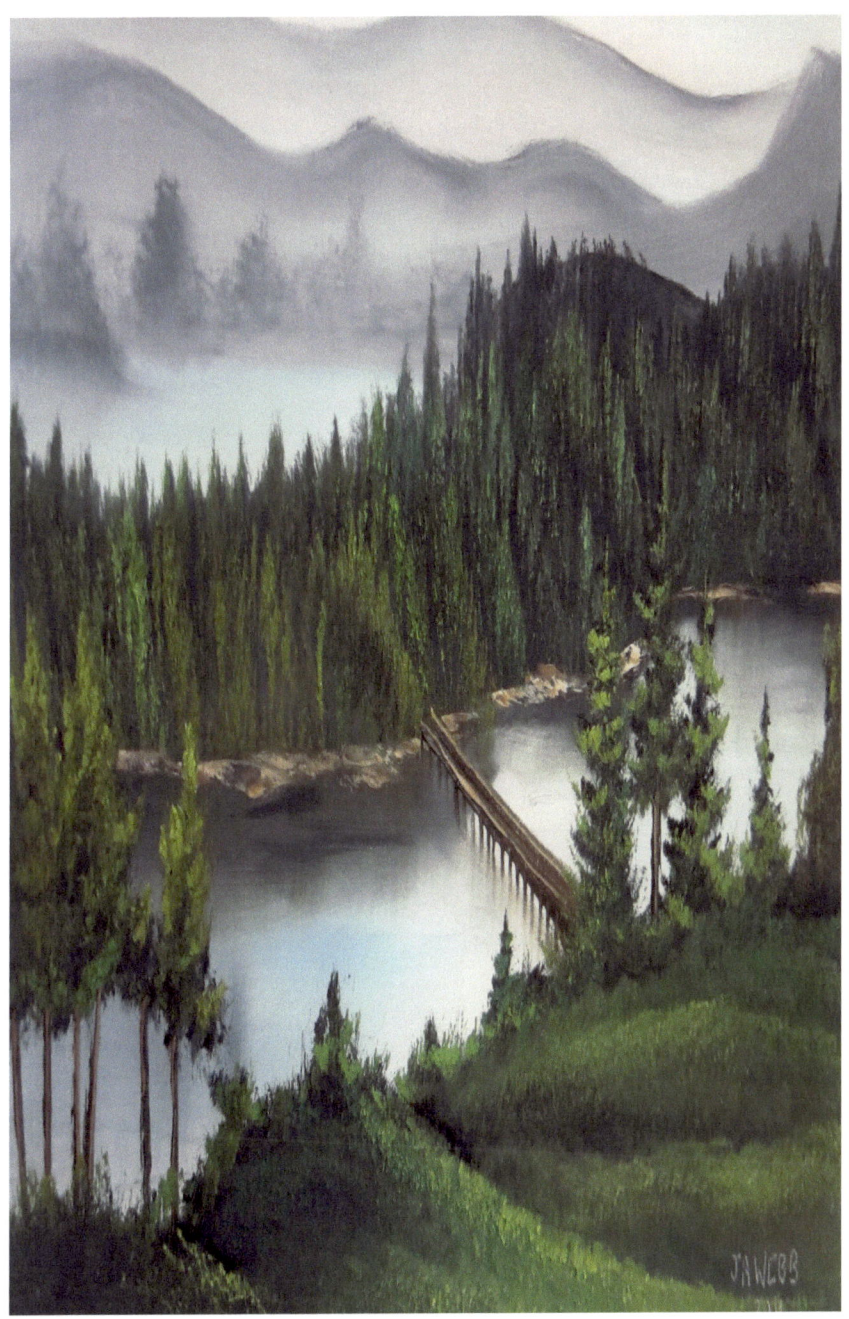

www.ingramcontent.com/pod-product-compliance
Lightning Source LLC
Chambersburg PA
CBHW041147180526
45159CB00002BB/746